# Water from a Tap

By Julie Haydon

Illustrations by Richard Morden

We drink water.

# Where does water come from?

Rain is water.

Rain falls from the clouds.

Some of the water goes into big lakes.

Water in the lakes
can be dirty.
We must not drink
dirty water.

The water from the lakes
runs along pipes
to a big cleaning station.

The water is cleaned
at the station.

Then pumps push
the clean water
into big pipes.

The big pipes are
under the ground.

Then the water goes into lots of small pipes.

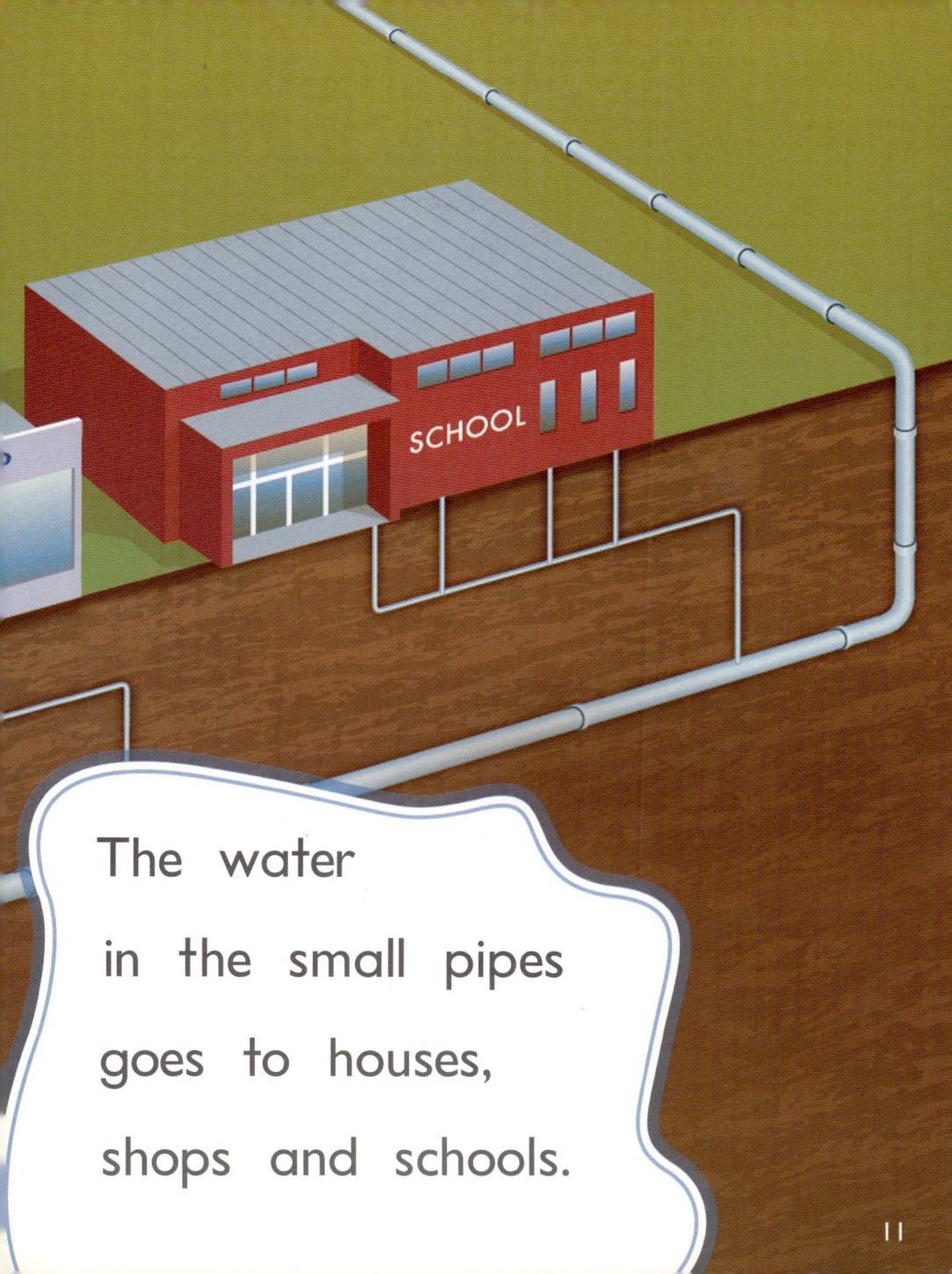

The water
in the small pipes
goes to houses,
shops and schools.

The water comes out
of the pipes
when a tap is turned on.

The water stops
when the tap is turned off.

We clean ourselves
with water.

We cook with water.

We all need water.

rain

lake

cleaning station

big pipe

SHOP

SCHOOL

small pipes

tap

16